CONTENTS

To access audio visit:
www.halleonard.com/mylibrary

Enter Code
3474-1668-1380-9566

Audio Arrangements by Peter Deneff

ISBN 978-1-4950-2304-0

HAL•LEONARD®
CORPORATION
7777 W. BLUEMOUND RD. P.O. BOX 13819 MILWAUKEE, WI 53213

Visit Hal Leonard Online at
www.halleonard.com

ALL ABOUT THAT BASS

TRUMPET

Words and Music by KEVIN KADISH
and MEGHAN TRAINOR

ALL OF ME

TRUMPET

Words and Music by JOHN STEPHENS
and TOBY GAD

HAPPY
from DESPICABLE ME 2

TRUMPET

Words and Music by
PHARRELL WILLIAMS

RADIOACTIVE

TRUMPET

Words and Music by DANIEL REYNOLDS,
BENJAMIN McKEE, DANIEL SERMON,
ALEXANDER GRANT and JOSH MOSSER

ROAR

TRUMPET

Words and Music by KATY PERRY,
LUKASZ GOTTWALD, MAX MARTIN,
BONNIE McKEE and HENRY WALTER

SAY SOMETHING

TRUMPET

Words and Music by IAN AXEL,
CHAD VACCARINO and MIKE CAMPBELL

SOMEONE LIKE YOU

Trumpet

Words and Music by ADELE ADKINS
and DAN WILSON

Slowly, with feeling

SHAKE IT OFF

TRUMPET

Words and Music by TAYLOR SWIFT,
MAX MARTIN and SHELLBACK

A SKY FULL OF STARS

TRUMPET

Words and Music by GUY BERRYMAN,
JON BUCKLAND, WILL CHAMPION,
CHRIS MARTIN and TIM BERGLING

THINKING OUT LOUD

TRUMPET

Words and Music by ED SHEERAN
and AMY WADGE

21

UPTOWN FUNK

TRUMPET

Words and Music by MARK RONSON,
BRUNO MARS, PHILIP LAWRENCE,
JEFF BHASKER, DEVON GALLASPY
and NICHOLAUS WILLIAMS

STAY WITH ME

TRUMPET

Words and Music by SAM SMITH,
JAMES NAPIER and WILLIAM EDWARD PHILLIPS